A Bark In The Park

A Guide For Walking Your Dog In Chester County

DOUG GELBERT

illustrations by

ANDREW CHESWORTH

CRUDEN BAY

About This Guide:

Have you ever considered how far you walk in a lifetime with your dog? If you walk just 20 minutes a day, in ten years you will have walked far enough to cover the United States coast to coast. With all that walking you are going to be on the lookout for variety.

This guide highlights 30 parks I refer to as "destination parks." These are not the local neighborhood parks where you go for your daily walk. I have selected 24 parks with trails within Chester County and another six in neighboring counties within a 30-minute drive of county borders.

Each park is rated on its desirability for dog-walking on a scale of one to four "hikers." These are my personal ratings and reflect my bias solely (Katie, my Border Collie/German Shepherd mix, would give them all four hikers). Roughly, they mean:

ONE HIKER	Not worth driving to.
TWO HIKERS	Worth stopping at if you're nearby.
THREE HIKERS	Worth driving to.
FOUR HIKERS	Worth planning a special dog/owner outing.

And, truth be told, any new trail is more exciting than even the most pleasant of familiar walks. So grab that leash and start walking!
DBG

•••

A BARK IN THE PARK

Copyright 2000 by Cruden Bay Books

All rights reserved. No part of this book may be reproduced or transmitted in any form or by any means, electronic or mechanical, including photocopying, recording or by any information storage and retrieval system without permission in writing from the Publisher.

Cruden Bay Books
PO Box 467
Montchanin, DE 19710

International Standard Book Number 0-9644427-3-6

Manufactured in the United States of America

INSIDE:

CHESTER COUNTY PARKS

PARKS NEARBY

Chester County Parks

AIRDRIE FOREST PRESERVE

THE PARK:

These woodlands, managed by the Open Land Conservancy, press against the northern edge of the commercial Paoli district. The original Airdrie Forest is in central Scotland, where legend has it witches and warlocks once roamed.

WALKS:

The trails in the preserve are on the east side of North Valley Road. All are walks through a wooded hillside overlooking a glen cut by a tributary of the Little Valley Creek.

TRAIL TIME?

Less than an hour.

TRAIL TERRAIN?

The trails slope as they drop towards the stream and the open field at the bottom of the hill.

TRAIL SURFACE?

Dirt.

TRAIL SENSE?

These trails are not marked and there is no map. The trails will dead-end at the edges of the preserve and at the stream and you will be retracing your steps at some point in your visit.

BONUS

Although you can just about reach the busy Main Line with a long leash, you can descend into these dark woods and instantly achieve a sense of seclusion.

SWIMMING?

Although the stream, a small branch of the Valley Creek, provides enough water for a quick drink, it is not deep enough for canine swimming.

ADMISSION FEE:

None.

PARK HOURS:

8:00 a.m. - sunset, year-round.

DIRECTIONS:

From Route 30 (Lancaster Avenue) turn onto North Valley Road, just east of the intersection with Paoli Pike. Make a right on Central Avenue and your second left on Fennerton Road. The entrance to the preserve is at the end of the lane.

No Dogs!

1. Battle of the Clouds Park
2. East Whiteland Township Preserve
3. Great Valley Nature Center
4. Jenkins Arboretum
5. Kardon Park
6. Kerr Park
7. Valley Creek Park

ANSON B. NIXON PARK

THE PARK:

The land here, featuring a 22-foot drop in the East Branch of the Red Clay Creek, was bought in 1795 by William Chambers to build a mill. He was looking to clean wool. Chambers named his property and fine mansion "Bloomfield," in honor of Brigadier General Bloomfield who drilled 3000 troops on his brother's adjoining property in prepartion for the War of 1812. The first organized school in the borough was conducted in a grove of trees here in 1830, a quarter-century before Kennett Square was incorporated. The property remained in the Chambers family for more than a century. The mansion burned and the 82-acre park was established in 1982.

WALKS:

The park is essentially carved into three main segments, each featuring a walking loop. The Beechwood Trail in the Beech Woods slips between rare umbrella magnolias, black gums and tupelos dressed in gnarly trunks deformed from a bacterial infection. Also here is the signature Kennett Beech which stood when William Penn came from England to claim his land grant more than 300 years ago. The Bloomfield Trail circumnavigates the small ponds at the center of the park. The Otherplace Trail, named for the home of Cyrus Chambers, penetrates the Pine Woods on the eastern side of the park. Informal spur trails also run through Nixon Park.

TRAIL TIME?

Less than one hour.

TRAIL TERRAIN?

Easy walking with only minor dips and rolls along the way.

TRAIL SURFACE?

Crushed gravel and hard-packed dirt, suitable for a stroller.

BONUS

A small remnant of the forests that blanketed southeastern Pennsylvania at the time of 17th century European settlement remain in the park. It retains the species diversity of the original woodland, with a mix of native trees rarely found in this area. The area's biodiversity is described on interpretive signs along the trails.

TRAIL SENSE?

The trails are unmarked but the many segments are short and any misdirection will not leave you lost for long. A painted map board is available in a kiosk in the parking lot.

SWIMMING?

The Red Clay Creek is not deep enough for anything beyond splashing. The ponds are set below the level of the trails, providing tricky access at times.

ADMISSION FEE:

None.

PARK HOURS:

7:00 a.m. - sunset, year-round.

DIRECTIONS:

The park is located in the northeast corner of Kennett Square. From Route 1, exit onto State Street and make a right at the bottom of Miller's Hill (the first one heading into town) onto N. Walnut Street. Make a left into the park at the fork 1/4 mile ahead. You can also access the park by taking Route 82 South from Route 1 and make your first left onto Leslie Road, past the Saint Patrick Cemetery. A small parking lot is by the ballfield at the end of the lane.

Dogs' lives are too short. Their only fault, really.

-Agnes Sligh Turnbull

BINKY LEE PRESERVE

THE PARK:

The Binky Lee Preserve, despite being pinched on all sides by development, seeks to retain the flavor of the 18th century farms which once dominated the Chester County landscape. The property was donated to Natural Lands Trust, who manage the land, in 1989.

WALKS:

Most of the walks here are through grassy meadowlands across a hillside with panoramic views of the countryside. A short woodlands trail at the top of the hill brings you into residential backyards and is actually less isolated than the trails through the open field. Some rock outcroppings are the main attraction of the wooded areas. You will also visit wetlands, forest restoration areas and successional areas on your walk.

TRAIL TIME?

Less than an hour.

TRAIL TERRAIN?

Binky Lee is situated across a wide, sloping hill necessitating easy to moderate climbs around the property.

TRAIL SURFACE?

Grass. The trails are mowed through the wild meadow grass.

TRAIL SENSE?

The trails are not marked. There is a trail map available in the office next to the barn, which dates from the late 1700s.

SWIMMING?

Pickering Creek slices through the corner of the property and is dammed into a shallow pond at one point. These wetlands don't provide much in the way of a doggie dip but are welcome on hot summer days.

BONUS

The trails are flanked by scores of birdhouses amidst the tall meadow grasses which provide ideal nesting habitat for a variety of birds including Eastern Bluebird, Bobolinks, Eastern Meadowlark and Redwinged Blackbirds.

ADMISSION FEE:

None.

PARK HOURS/PHONE:

8:00 a.m.-sunset, year round. (610.827.0156)

DIRECTIONS:

Binky Lee Preserve is in West Pikeland Township, southwest of Phoenixville. Travelling on Route 113 towards Phoenixville, make a right on Pikeland Road opposite from the sign for "Historic Yellow Springs." The entrance to the preserve is on the left, after about 3/4 of a mile. Continue straight on the entrance road, make a right past the barn and park in the grassy area up the hill.

BLACK ROCK PRESERVE

THE PARK:

North of Phoenixville, the Schuylkill River bends back on itself, forming a thumb of land containing Black Rock Preserve. In 1995 Chester County won federal funding to acquire and restore 133 acres of the Black Rock Silt Basin for the preservation of diverse bird species.

WALKS:

A linear trail hugs the Schuylkill River for nearly a mile and continues for another mile outside the preserve below Black Rock Dam. The dam is a stone-filled timber crib structure 11 feet high and 370 feet long. It is one of 32 dams built on the Schuylkill River to aid navigation on the 108-mile Schuylkill Canal. A narrow trail on an elevated berm circumnavigates the small impounding area in the preserve.

TRAIL TIME?

Less than one hour.

TRAIL TERRAIN?

The trails are flat but the connecting trails between the marsh walk and the river walk are steep, albeit short.

TRAIL SURFACE?

Grass and soft dirt trails easily become mud as they are on the same elevation as the river. The trail between the canal and the river below the dam has many embedded rocks.

TRAIL SENSE?

The trails are not marked and no map or signs are available, but there is also no place to wander from the trails.

SWIMMING?

There is excellent access to the Schuylkill River in the 3-mile dam pool and good swimming in the marsh as well.

BONUS

Across the Schuylkill River, upstream from Black Rock Dam, is a rocky crag which towers 100 feet over the water and carries the following 19th century lore: "A stunted cedar grew upon the very verge and it made the most masculine heart tremble to stand upon the edge and while clinging to this frail support look down into the waters beneath. Sometime after the settlement when the natives had been in contact with the whites long enough to acquire their vices an Indian was tempted with the promise of a bottle of whiskey to leap three times from this crag into the river. Twice he made the terrible plunge successfully. Returning after the second attempt wearied with the unwanted exertion and bleeding from wounds made by some sharp stones against which he had struck he sprang again into the stream never more to appear." Since that time it has borne the name of Indian Rock.

ADMISSION FEE:

None.

PARK HOURS:

Sunrise - sunset, year-round.

DIRECTIONS:

The preserve is in northeast Phoenixville, on Route 113 (Black Rock Road). There is a small, unmarked parking lot at Black Rock Dam (past a solitary green mailbox on the right) and a larger lot at the bridge crossing the Schuylkill River.

No one appreciates the very special genius of your conversation as a dog does.

-Christopher Morley

CROW'S NEST PRESERVE

THE PARK:

Most of the woods in this area were sacrificed to the charcoal kilns of the early American iron industry. Four of the 19th century farms located here were consolidated into one in the 1950s and that farm was subsequently donated to the National Lands Trust is 1991. Today, the leased fields produce corn, wheat and hay. The Crow's Nest Preserve covers 600 acres.

WALKS:

The trails are connecting linear affairs which can be combined in many ways for your afternoon's hike. The Creek Trail is exceptionally beautiful; flat, wide and soft along a narrow and twisting French Creek, flowing just miles from its source on the way to the Schuylkill River. The Hopewell Trail is a wooded jaunt connecting to the exceedingly pleasant Bethesda Church Trail in Hopewell Furnace National Historic Site.

TRAIL TIME?

More than an hour.

TRAIL TERRAIN?

The rolling hills sport some moderate climbs which lead to impressive views across the corn and wheat.

TRAIL SURFACE?

Mostly dirt and grass; beware on the Farm Fields Trail which is sometimes cut from the crop stalks, leaving tiny spears that can injure a pet's paws.

TRAIL SENSE?

The trails are marked but not always distinct when the blazes are on young trees in regenerating woods. The best trail map in Chester County is available.

BONUS

American Indians frequently visited the headwaters of the French Creek and occasionally settled here. Local lore indicates that the burial place of an important chief is located on the property. A loop off the Creek Trail visits Chief's Grove.

SWIMMING?

The French Creek is just for splashing; there is no trail access to the ponds on the property.

ADMISSION FEE:

None.

PARK HOURS/PHONE:

8:00 a.m. - sunset, year-round. (610.286.7955)

DIRECTIONS:

From Route 23, turn north on Trythall Road (1.3 miles west of Knauertown and marked by a sign for Warwick Woods Campground). Follow Trythall Road until it deadends at Harmonyville Road. Turn left onto Harmonyville Road and then take the first right at Piersol Road. The parking area is on the left in the field past the barn/visitor center.

DIAMOND ROCK PRESERVE

THE PARK:

Diamond Rock Preserve is a tract of land squeezed between the Pennsylvania Turnpike and emerging developments, managed by the Open Land Conservancy.

WALKS:

The entire preserve is heavily wooded and although there is some interesting topography, you can never escape the feeling that you are walking in someone's backyard. And unless one of those backyards is yours, there is no reason to come here.

TRAIL TIME?

Less than an hour.

TRAIL TERRAIN?

The trails slope as they move along the top of a ridge.

TRAIL SURFACE?

Dirt.

TRAIL SENSE?

There trails are not marked and there is no map. Several of the trails narrow to the point of disappearing - follow your dog's nose!

SWIMMING?

There is not a drop of water at Diamond Rock Preserve.

ADMISSION FEE:

None.

PARK HOURS:

8:00 a.m. - sunset, year-round.

BONUS

Segments of the Horse-Shoe Trail, which stretches for 133 miles from Valley Forge to Hershey, have been in use since the mid-1700s, beginning as a trail linking the numerous iron ore forges and furnaces along its route. Established in 1935, the Horse-Shoe Trail ("Horse" for riders, "Shoe" for hikers) is unique in that it was built for equestrian and pedestrian travel. However, today, it lacks continuous access to public land and must often share the right of way with automobile roads in Chester County. One place you can walk in peace is through Diamond Rock Preserve.

DIRECTIONS:

Diamond Rock Preserve is in Tredyffrin Township, east of Valley Forge. Travelling north on Route 29, make a right on Yellow Springs Road. Take your first left on Howells Road and your third right onto Chautauqua Trail. Park in the neighborhood circle and follow the construction roads to the preserve on your right.

EXTON PARK/CHESTER VALLEY TRAIL

THE PARK:

In June 1994, Chester County and West Whiteland Township combined to jointly purchase 727 acres of land in heavily developed eastern Chester County. Under development, the Township park will accommodate active recreation and the County park will seek to develop trails through the wooded slopes and transitional meadow.

The Chester Valley Trail project dates to 1991 and seeks to develop an abandoned rail line into a 16-mile bike-and-hike trail between Downingtown and Norristown. The initial one-mile segment of the trail, the southern boundary of Exton Park, opened on June 3, 2000, National Trails Day.

WALKS:

While the Exton Park is under development there is an informal trail circumnavigating a pond on the property. The Chester Valley Trail here is through an open field. The shade along the trail is sparse for your four-legged friend, who is less tolerant of the heat than we are. The trail is cut beneath the surface of the field and there is not much of a view.

TRAIL TIME?

Less than an hour.

TRAIL TERRAIN?

There is a slight grade to the old rail line, which is all but imperceptable.

BONUS

Ever want to design your own park? Given a piece of land, what would you do? Landscape the lake? Build the trails? How would you make the park dog-friendly? Here is your chance to let your imagination off the leash as you walk along through this embryonic park.

TRAIL SURFACE?

The Chester Valley Trail is crushed stone and dirt.

TRAIL SENSE?

The old rail line doesn't require any.

SWIMMING?

The reed-encircled pond provides good swimming; there is a small pond off the Chester Valley Trail but you have to work to get at it.

ADMISSION FEE:

None.

PARK HOURS:

8 a.m. - sunset, year-round.

DIRECTIONS:

From Route 100, take Swedesford Road east. Parking as of this writing is still on grass, at the park sign. You can also park on the grass along Church Farm School Lane at the Chester Valley Trail.

My dog can bark like a Congressman, fetch like an aide, beg like a press secretary and play dead like a receptionist.

-Gerald Solomon

FRENCH CREEK STATE PARK

THE PARK:

A wilderness fort once stood on the small stream flowing through these woods which was garrisoned by the French during the French and Indian War and thus "French Creek." The hillsides here were dotted with charcoal hearths throughout the 1800s, fueling the nascent American iron industry. French Creek State Park was originally developed by the federal government during the Depression as a National Park Service Demonstration Area. Civilian Conservation Corps members, organized by President Franklin Roosevelt, built dams, roads and other recreational trappings. In 1946, the area was transferred to the Commonwealth of Pennsylvania.

WALKS:

Approximately 40 miles of trails visit every corner of French Creek's 7,339 acres. There are 8 featured hikes of between one and four hours' duration. The marquee walk is the Boone Trail, a six-mile loop connecting all the major attractions of the park. All the walks are heavily forested with hardwoods - keep an eye out for the ruins of the area's charcoal-burning past.

TRAIL TIME?

More than an hour.

TRAIL TERRAIN?

There are many steep sections as you ramble about these wooded hills.

TRAIL SURFACE?

Dirt with frequent rocky stretches, especially on the slopes. Some trails make use of fire roads.

TRAIL SENSE?

All the trails sport distinct colored blazes. A trail map is available and you would be well advised to take it as the trailheads and junctions are not named.

BONUS

Considered by some as the "Orienteering Capital of North America," French Creek has developed a permanent self-guided course for the practioners of the art of map and compass. You can even challenge your dog's nose in a wayfinding contest.

SWIMMING?

There is abundant access to two lakes, the 21-acre cold water Scotts Run Lake and the 63-acre Hopewell Lake.

ADMISSION FEE:

None.

PARK HOURS/PHONE:

8:00 a.m. - sunset, year-round. (610.582.9680)

DIRECTIONS:

French Creek State Park is located north of Elverson. From Route 23, take Route 345 North to the south entrance of the park on the left. From the Pennsylvania Turnpike the park is 7 miles northeast of the Morgantown Interchange (Exit 22).

HIBERNIA COUNTY PARK

THE PARK:

The first property deeds in this area date to October 1, 1765. In the 1790s, Samuel Downing built the first iron forge at Hibernia, along the West Branch of the Brandywine Creek. Downing lost his forge in a sheriff's sale in 1808 and the property rapidly passed through many owners until Charles Brooke purchased the enterprise in 1821. He then expanded its holdings to 1,710 acres. By the Civil War, the Hibernia Iron Works was churning pig iron into bar iron from two forges, two heating furnaces and a rolling mill.

The forge went silent in the 1870s. In 1894, Colonel Franklin Swayne, a successful Philadelphia real estate lawyer, purchased the property and transformed Hibernia (the Roman name for Ireland) into a gentleman's country estate. A long-time admirer of the English manor tradition, Colonel Swayne made 29 trips to the British countryside to collect ideas for his home. On one such trip he purchased the massive lion heads which adorn the pillar gate posts. It was the colonel who is thought to have covered the stone exterior of the mansion with its distinctive coppery peach stucco. In 1963 the old ironmaster's mansion and nearly 900 acres of surrounding grounds passed to Chester County for renovation as a park.

WALKS:

Hibernia features 5 main trails, all wooded and none longer than 1.5 miles. Only the Cedar Hollow Trail loops so you will need to combine park roads and unmarked paths to avoid retracing steps in your walking day. One unmarked trail at the end of the Forge Trail hugs the Brandywine Creek for nearly a mile - one of the longest waterside walks in Chester County.

TRAIL TIME?

More than an hour.

BONUS

The greatest tree in the Colonial forest was the American Chestnut. Struck down by a pandemic chestnut blight in the 1930s, full-grown specimens of the tree have become nearly extinct. Some hardy shoots have survived here but as they mature, they too will fall victim to the fatal blight.

TRAIL TERRAIN?

Most of the walking is easy; there are slight hills down to the Brandywine and the Rim Trail across the creek requires a good climb to reach the ridge.

TRAIL SURFACE?

Most trails are dirt; the Lake Trail is paved with crushed stone.

TRAIL SENSE?

The trailheads are marked but some of the trails are more energetically marked than others. Do not let go of the trail map if you attempt to find the Rim Trail.

SWIMMING?

Dogs can enjoy a dip in the Brandywine Creek, a fishing pond or Chambers Lake - a 90-acre water reservoir created in 1994 with the damming of Birch Run.

ADMISSION FEE:

None.

PARK HOURS/PHONE:

Sunrise - sunset, year-round. (610.383.3812)

DIRECTIONS:

Hibernia Park is four miles north of Coatesville. From Route 30, Take Route 82 North two miles to Cedar Knoll Road, turn left and travel 1.25 miles to the main entrance.

HOPEWELL FURNACE NATIONAL HISTORIC SITE

THE PARK:

Mark Bird built Hopewell Furnace here in 1771, an area rich in hardwoods and rushing water. By the time of the Revolution five years later, Hopewell and other American furnaces, forges and mills were producing one-seventh of the world's iron goods. Hopewell today is a restoration of an 1820s iron plantation and the community which thrived in its shadow.

WALKS:

Hopewell features several well-maintained hiking trails, most far from the visitors of the Historic Area. The two Chester County hikes at the site are the Bethesda Church Trail and a segment of the Horse-Shoe Trail. Both are heavily wooded linear trails. The Lenape Trail begins on Hopewell Road and connects to French Creek State Park.

TRAIL TIME?

More than one hour.

TRAIL TERRAIN?

Some moderate climbs on the rolling land, which is seldom flat.

TRAIL SURFACE?

The dirt trails are wide and well-manicured.

TRAIL SENSE?

The trails are blazed and a site map is available.

Any man who does not like dogs and want them does not deserve to be in the White House.

-Calvin Coolidge

BONUS

For the ambitious dog who wants to do more with his sticks than fetch and chew, there are demonstrations on charcoal-making by costumed interpreters in the Historic Area.

SWIMMING?

The creeks are shallow and not a prominent feature of hikes at Hopewell.

ADMISSION FEE:

None.

PARK HOURS/PHONE:

Sunrise - sunset, year-round. (610.582.8773)

DIRECTIONS:

Hopewell Furnace is five miles south of Birdsboro on Route 345. The main parking lot is for the benefit of the visitors to the Historic Area and does not provide ready access to the trails. Depending on your hiking itinerary you may be better served walking into Hopewell from a connecting trail in Crow's Nest Preserve or French Creek State Park.

Best Parks To Take The Dog Swimming

1. French Creek State Park
2. Hibernia County Park
3. Marsh Creek State Park
4. Valley Forge National Historical Park
5. Lorimer Nature Preserve

LORIMER NATURE PRESERVE

THE PARK:

This nature preserve, managed by the Open Land Conservancy, seems to be the prototype for protecting land against overdevelopment. While the trails are quiet, never do you achieve a sense of isolation from the surrounding communities.

WALKS:

The Lorimer Preserve is an ideal spot for a walk of a half-hour or less. The short, interconnecting trails offer a nice mix of fields and woods on your hike and two delightful ponds are available for a quick doggie dip.

TRAIL TIME?

Less than an hour.

TRAIL TERRAIN?

Easy walking throughout with many flat stretches, especially in the fields; the woodlands offer some tumbling terrain but no serious climbs.

TRAIL SURFACE?

Dirt and grass.

TRAIL SENSE?

There are no maps and no blazed trails so your route is left to your imagination. You can criss-cross the property and still find your way back to the car without calling for a rescue party.

SWIMMING?

The two ponds on the property are fantastic for canine aquatics, especially the smaller of the two, tucked into a hollow in the woods. Your dog can swim across the pond while you race him to the other side by circling the water on land.

BONUS

Born in Louisville, Kentucky in 1868, George Horace Lorimer kicked around working in a meat-packing company and as a retail grocer before turning to reporting. In 1899 Lorimer was hired as literary editor of the *Saturday Evening Post* and was soon promoted to editor-in-chief. It was the last job he would ever have. Before his retirement in 1936 Lorimer raised circulation from 1,800 to over three million. Among his discoveries was a 22-year old artist whose work he bought immediately upon seeing and for 45 years Norman Rockwell contributed covers to the *Post*. Lorimer, a resident of Wyncote, was a passionate conservationist during his lifetime and this preserve is named in his honor.

ADMISSION FEE:

None.

PARK HOURS:

Sunrise - sunset, year-round.

DIRECTIONS:

Lorimer Nature Preserve is in Tredyffrin Township. The main entrance is on North Valley Road, north of Swedesford Road. Turn right into the small parking lot up the hill from the bridge across Valley Creek.

Ever consider what they must think of us? I mean, here we come back from the grocery store with the most amazing haul - chicken, pork, half a cow...They must think we're the greatest hunters on earth!

-Anne Tyler

MARSH CREEK STATE PARK

THE PARK:

To counter frequent flooding in the Brandywine Creek watershed, plans for Marsh Creek Dam began in 1955. Work on the 89-foot earthen dam began in 1970. In 1974 the lake began to fill and six months later 535 acres of what used to be Milford Mills were under up to 73 feet of water. Gone were 42 residences and more than 70 old barns and other structures.

WALKS:

Marsh Creek Lake dominates the 1,705 acres of the park. There is no hiking at the main entrance on the east side of the lake. All the hiking - six miles worth - lies on the western shores. The main loop (Bridle Trail) is interjected with three inner loops. The trail is on a hill overlooking the lake but water views are few. The trails are heavily wooded.

TRAIL TIME:

More than an hour.

TRAIL TERRAIN?

Hilly leading from the trailhead but easy walking once the high hill is scaled; down the opposite side of the hill the trail hooks into an old railbed along the East Branch of the Brandywine Creek. This stretch of trail, the prettiest in the park, is flat.

BONUS

Theodore Burr built a bridge spanning the Hudson River at Waterford, New York in 1804. He added an arch segment to the multiple truss bridge popular at the time, attaining a longer span. Patented in 1817, the Burr Arch Truss became one of the most common in the construction of covered bridges. The Larkin's Bridge, a 65-foot long, 45-ton "Burr Arch" covered bridge erected in 1854 and rebuilt in 1881, was relocated to the northeast section of the park in 1972. Larkin's Covered Bridge is the only remaining legacy of Milford Mills.

TRAIL SURFACE?

Mostly dirt although there are long stretches of rocky trail on the slopes which are tough on foot and paw.

TRAIL SENSE?

There are many more trails at Marsh Creek State Park than are indicated on the trail map. An occasional sign pops up to inspire confidence and some blazes but mostly you and the dog are on your own.

SWIMMING?

Accessed from the parking lot, Marsh Creek Lake offers the best lake swimming in Chester County; the Brandywine Creek here is usually too shallow for anything more than splashing.

ADMISSION FEE:

None.

PARK HOURS/PHONE:

8:00 a.m. - sunset, year-round. (610.458.5119)

DIRECTIONS:

The hiking trails at Marsh Creek are reached from Route 282 (Creek Road). From the south, make a right on Reeds Road North. From the north, make a left on Lyndell Road. Both feed into Marsh Creek Road and the parking lot.

NOTTINGHAM COUNTY PARK

THE PARK:

Although this area had already been settled for nearly two centuries, it was not until 1828 that serpentinite was discovered in what is now Nottingham Park. By 1880 the Wood Mine dug to extract the mineral was 800 feet deep and the largest in the world. Chrome, asbestos and quartz were also mined here. The oldest of Chester County's parks, Nottingham was dedicated in 1963.

WALKS:

There are 8 trails in Nottingham Park, which can all be covered in a day's hiking. Most of the trails criss-cross and do not loop, often just running out at the boundaries of the 600-acre park. Look for the "Mystery Hole," an abandoned mine now filled with water.

TRAIL TIME?

More than an hour.

TRAIL TERRAIN?

The rolling hills through the park can be formidable at times.

TRAIL SURFACE?

Natural surface with dirt, sand and rocks.

TRAIL SENSE?

The trails are blazed and named but study the available maps closely so you don't follow a trail to a dead-end at the back of the park without creating a loop. You will often be confronted with signposts at trail junctions. Choose wisely.

SWIMMING?

McPherson Lake and Little Pond are open-field swimming holes for a doggie dip.

ADMISSION FEE:

None.

BONUS

Nottingham Park is home to the Serpentine Barrens, a seven-mile ridge of igneous rock that is one of only three such serpentine formations in Noth America. The early settlers called the area of scrub pine and oak "barrens" because its low nutrient-level was unfriendly to cultivation. The distinctive green serpentine rock was a popular building stone and can be seen in many of Chester County's historic structures, including several at West Chester University. An interpretive nature trail describes the fast-draining Serpentine Barrens and visits abandoned quarries.

PARK HOURS/PHONE:

Sunrise - sunset, year-round. (610.932.2589)

DIRECTIONS:

Nottingham County Park is just north of the Pennsylvania-Maryland state line. Take Route 1 South and exit on Route 272, crossing back over the highway to the entrance of Herr's Snack Foods on the right. Make a right when you can turn left to the Herr's Factory and another right (Park Road) to the parking lot on the left.

Best Parks To Walk The Dog And Push The Baby Stroller

1. Valley Forge National Historical Park
2. Struble Hike-Bike Trail
3. Anson B. Nixon Park
4. Chester Valley Trail

OAKBURNE PARK

THE PARK:

John Hulme built the first granite shelter on this land, selecting the highest area on the property for his homesite. In 1882 a wealthy Philadelphia lawyer named James Smith purchased 143 acres of land on the west side of South Concord Road, including Hulme's house. Smith renamed it "Oakburne" and set more than 150 skilled craftsmen to work refurbishing his new summer home. Oakburne was soon the centerpiece of a 27-acre park with fountains, miniature lakes and rustic bridges. Oakburne even had its own private railroad station and post office.

Oakburne was willed out of the Smith family to the Philadelphia Protestant Episcopal City Mission in 1896 for the operation of a convalescent home for women over 21 years of age. The next 70 years saw thousands of female "guests" treated here before its costly operation overwhelmed its directors. Westtown Township saved Oakburne from developers in 1974, eventually creating a 90-acre park.

WALKS:

Three connecting trails (Creek, Nature and Park) form a loop of nearly three miles to visit all areas of the park on both sides of Concord Road. The trails are all wooded, including native specimens and the remains of the Smiths' exotic plantings around the mansion.

TRAIL TIME:

More than an hour.

TRAIL TERRAIN?

There are some dips and rolls in some of the wooded areas, including one good climb on the Creek Trail.

TRAIL SURFACE?

Dirt and grass , with stretches of sand and rocks underfoot.

BONUS

The most striking feature of the estate was a 1,000-gallon, twin-tank water tower built on the lawn away from the mansion. Built of stone and brick to resemble a fortress, the tower features dormer-style twin roofs. James Smith installed the finest of telescopes at Oakburne that offered views across the countryside of Chester and Philadelphia.

TRAIL SENSE?

The trails are haphazardly marked in places (the blazes are the smallest in Chester County) and can be hard to follow, especially picking the trail up across Concord Road. A map board is available between the parking lot and the mansion.

SWIMMING?

Part of the trail hopscotches past Chester Creek but, while scenic, it offers little opportunity for swimming, save for one deep hole under the railroad bridge. One of Smith's miniature lakes, encircled by reeds, is a pleasant canine swimming stop.

ADMISSION FEE:

None.

PARK HOURS:

Sunrise - sunset, year-round.

DIRECTIONS:

Oakburne Park is in Westtown Township. Coming south on Route 202, make a left on Matlack Street, which runs into Oakburne Road and South Concord Road. Make a right into the driveway and proceed past the mansion to the parking lot. Coming north on Route 202, make a right on Route 926 (Street Road) and a left on Concord Road. The park is on the left.

Money will buy a pretty good dog but it won't buy the wag of his tail.

-Josh Billings

SHARP'S/CANTERBURY WOODS

THE PARK:

This 28-acre preserve, a part of the Natural Lands Trust, is located in the midst of a heavy residential area.

WALKS:

The wide, well-maintained trails total 2.5 miles and criss-cross the property many times. The abundant trail segments do not loop and often times you pop out in a back yard or at a road.

TRAIL TIME?

Less than one hour.

TRAIL TERRAIN?

These trails are all flat.

TRAIL SURFACE?

Many soft grass trails and some dirt trails; some are laced with heavy exposed roots in spots.

TRAIL SENSE?

None of the trails is marked.

SWIMMING?

There are small wet meadows and shallow streams but no ponds and no suitable place for swimming.

ADMISSION FEE:

None.

PARK HOURS:

Sunrise - sunset, year-round.

<u>BONUS</u>

With the small trees and shrubs overhanging the trail in many places, the short segments give this walk the feel of an English maze garden.

DIRECTIONS:

From the intersection of Routes 30 and 252 in Paoli, travel south on Route 252 for approximately 1.5 miles to Leopard Road. Turn left onto Leopard and proceed .5 miles to Byrd Drive. Turn left onto Byrd Drive and proceed 100 yards to the Sharp's Woods sign on the right. There is no parking lot; only street parking along Byrd Drive and Argyle Road.

We are alone, absolutely alone on this chance planet; and, amid all the forms of life that surround us, not one, excepting the dog, has made an alliance with us.

-Maurice Maeterlinck

SPRINGTON MANOR FARM

THE PARK:

Springton Manor was originally an 8,313 acre parcel set aside by William Penn in 1701. The land has been farmed for almost three centuries and lives today as a demonstration farm. A small forge also operated here for much of the 18th century. Abraham McIlvaine built the main house in 1833. Springton Manor Farm is listed on the National Register of Historic Places for its importance in architecture, agriculture and conservation.

WALKS:

The Indian Run Trail loops around the entire property - evenly divided between field and woods hiking. In July the southwestern edge of the field is bursting with the most accessible red raspberries in Chester County. There is also available a 1/3-mile Penn Oak Interpretive Nature Trail.

TRAIL TIME?

More than an hour.

TRAIL TERRAIN?

The farmland sweeps down a long hillside providing gentle climbs and sparkling views; the lowlands surrounding Indian Run are flat.

TRAIL SURFACE?

The Indian Run loop is dirt and grass with some wood chips under foot; the Nature Trail is paved with macadam.

TRAIL SENSE?

The loop is the only trail on the property. Although it is not marked, it is easy to follow. There is a map available.

SWIMMING?

The Farmer's Pond, at the edge of the Nature Trail, was built in 1896 as an additional water source for crops and livestock. The shallow-running Indian Run is good for splashing.

BONUS

Liberated from their sun-stealing neighbors of the crowded woods, the "King" and "Queen" White Oaks have spread out into a massive canopy of leaves. The "Queen" measures seventeen feet around at the thickest part of the trunk and the "King" is closer to twenty. The two trees are part of the "Penn's Woods" collection of 139 trees standing when William Penn arrived to survey his Pennsylvania colony. The arboreal oldsters reside at the last stop of the nature trail.

ADMISSION FEE:

None.

PARK HOURS/PHONE:

8:00 a.m. - sunset, year-round. (610.942.2450)

DIRECTIONS:

Springton Manor is northwest of Downingtown. Take Route 282, Creek Road, out of Downingtown for five miles and make a left on Springton Road. The entrance to the park is up the hill on the left.

STATE GAME LANDS NO. 43

THE PARK:

Three segments of these public lands, totalling 2,150 acres, lie in northwest Chester County. The most accessible - and scenic - of the three is at Saint Peters. Once known as the Falls of French Creek and a famous local tourist destination, Saint Peters was named for the town church when the post office moved away.

WALKS:

The Horse-Shoe Trail cuts through the Saint Peters and Pine Swamp Tracts. The Saint Peters walk is heavily wooded; the Pine Swamp walk leads through a scruffy meadow on old access roads through light woods at the edge of fields. There are many other short interconnecting trails at Saint Peters.

TRAIL TIME:

More than an hour.

TRAIL TERRAIN?

The rolling terrain never gets oppressive and the walking is easy throughout.

TRAIL SURFACE?

Dirt.

TRAIL SENSE?

The Horse-Shoe Trail is blazed but there is no trail map to untwine the maze of trails under the trees at Saint Peters. The Horse-Shoe Trail has no branches as it slices through the Pine Swamp tract.

SWIMMING?

French Creek rushes downhill through the property, pooling into an ideal swimming pond just south of the parking lot. Pine Creek can be accessed at Pine Swamp from the bridge near the parking lot.

BONUS

Forty million years ago an igneous explosion occurred underground here and cooled very quickly leaving behind a particularly fine granite rock. Tourists and students of geology alike made the pilgrimmage to the Falls of French Creek to study the rock formations. Granite quarries mined the rock and granite from Saint Peters once received an award at the 1893 World's Columbian Exposition in Chicago as "a fine-grained polished cube, a good building and ornamental stone." The quarries closed in the 1960s and many pits can still be seen. Today the giant boulders in French Creek are ideal for your dog to sramble on - or just lie in the sun.

ADMISSION FEE:

None.

PARK HOURS:

Sunrise - sunset, year-round.

DIRECTIONS:

The parking lot at Saint Peters is on Saint Peters Road, north of Route 23 (Ridge Road). It is behind the buildings on the left, at the northern edge of town. In Pine Swamp there is a small, unmarked parking lot on Harmonyville Road, east of Route 345 (Pine Swamp Road).

If you pick up a starving dog and make him prosperous, he will not bite you. This is the principal difference between a dog and a man.

-Mark Twain

STROUD PRESERVE

THE PARK:

This corner of Chester County was dominated by the Elmsley Farm, owned for seven successive generations by the Jefferis and James families from 1712 to 1938. The area is today a recognized historic district.

Formerly the Georgia Farm, the Stroud Preserve was given to the Natural Lands Trust by Dr. Morris W. Stroud to protect and preserve some of the rolling hills and farmland of Chester County. Although the preserve's more than 575 acres straddle Creek Road, the hiking is only on the west side of the road.

WALKS:

Fifteen miles of old farm and service roads criss-cross the property, many cresting in sweeping hilltop vistas of the surrounding countryside. Trails wind through the farm fields and lunge into the occasional hardwood parcel.

TRAIL TIME?

More than one hour.

TRAIL TERRAIN?

Rolling hills provide long, but moderate ascents and descents throughout the back of the property; the entrance road to the main barn is flat.

TRAIL SURFACE?

Mostly dirt roads, some stone-studded roads and some grass paths.

TRAIL SENSE?

The trails do not loop and are not marked. The roads all run off the property at one point or another and you will need the available trail map if you want to know where you are going to wind up. If you just want to ramble and explore, the wide open ground makes orientation easy.

BONUS

Early barns in Chester County were hastily thrown together of neccessity with logs. In English tradition they were small, one-floor storage bins for hay and grain. As the fields were cleared of the limestone, granite and red sandstone there was abundant building material for more permanent barns. Pennsylvania's oldest remaining barn, a handsome stone structure circa 1724, stands just north of the parking lot at Stroud Preserve. Compare this with the massive structure at the preserve headquarters, typical of the historic barns sunken into one of Chester Countys'southeastward-facing slopes to guarantee warmth in the winter.

SWIMMING?

Pleasant ponds dot the preserve but the best swimming is in a tranquil stretch of the East Branch of the Brandywine Creek.

ADMISSION FEE:

None.

PARK HOURS/PHONE:

8:00 a.m. - sunset, year-round. (610.696.6187)

DIRECTIONS:

Stroud Preserve is west of West Chester. Take Route 162 (Strasburg Road) for two miles and make a left on Creek Road. The small dirt parking lot - which is not marked - is about 1/2 mile on the left. Entrance to the preserve is across Creek Road.

Dog. A kind of additional or subidiary Deity designed to catch the overflow and surplus of the world's worship.

-Ambrose Bierce

ROBERT G. STRUBLE HIKE-BIKE TRAIL

THE PARK:

Created from an abandoned Pennsylvania Railroad line in 1979, the Struble Trail will eventually connect Downingtown with Honey Brook Borough - a total of 16 miles. As of this writing, 2.5 miles are completed, stretching northward from the end of Kardon Park's Lion's Trail in Downingtown. The trail is named for Robert Struble, a noted Chester County conservationist.

WALKS:

The 10-foot wide multi-use trail parallels the East Branch of the Brandywine Creek. It is wooded for most of its length and is especially scenic above the Dowlin Forge Road parking area. There are short, unimproved spurs off the main trail which dead-end quickly or lead to the water's edge. A pleasant side trail leads to Jones Pond and Dowlin Forge Park.

TRAIL TIME?

More than an hour.

BONUS

Samuel Hibbard started the first forge in Uwchlan Township in 1785. By 1801, the forge was in the Dowlin family and when Norris Dowlin married Mary Ann Lewis it became known as the Mary Ann Forge. Here pig iron was molded into strap hinges, hooks scythes and horseshoe plates. In full flourish the site boasted a stone stable, stone and log coal houses, three log dwellings and a smith shop to complement the forge. Remains are still visible, including the mill race which brought water from the Brandywine to power the operation.

TRAIL TERRAIN?

There is very little grade in the old rail line.

TRAIL SURFACE?

Crushed stone topped with oil; the trail to Dowlin Forge Park is also paved.

TRAIL SENSE?

Stay on the paved surface and remember which way you are going and you will never get lost.

SWIMMING?

The Brandywine Creek and a refreshing doggie dip is never more than a few steps away. Be considerate of the many fishermen who ply these waters.

ADMISSION FEE:

None.

PARK HOURS:

Dawn to dusk.

DIRECTIONS:

The Struble Trail entrance and parking lot is off Route 282 on Norwood Road in Downingtown. There is also a small lot opposite Dowlin Forge Road near the middle of the trail.

VALLEY CREEK PRESERVE

THE PARK:

These lowlands, dominated by the meanderings of the Valley Creek, are managed by the Open Land Conservancy.

WALKS:

The reedy walks are lightly wooded. When the vegetation is hardy, the paths can be narrow. The path follows the Valley Creek, emerging onto a duck pond.

TRAIL TIME?

Less than an hour.

TRAIL TERRAIN?

Mostly flat.

TRAIL SURFACE?

Dirt and grass, which can be exceedingly muddy in wet times. This is not the walk to take after a heavy rain.

TRAIL SENSE?

There is only one trail that runs from one end of the preserve to the other, with little variation. The trail is not marked and no map is available.

BONUS

Valley Creek manages to convey a secluded feeling in a residential area. The time here is more of a garden walk than a hike.

SWIMMING?

The pretty Valley Creek is not consistently deep enough for sustained swims but you will be hard-pressed to keep a water-loving dog on its banks.

ADMISSION FEE:

None.

PARK HOURS:

Dawn to dusk.

DIRECTIONS:

Valley Creek Preseve is north of Paoli. From Route 30, take North Valley Road north across Swedesford Road and make a left on Tree Line Road. Access to the Preserve is at the end. From Swedesford Road, turn onto Wisteria Drive, which loops at the end. At the back of the loop make a right onto Hayfield. An entrance to the preserve is at the circle at the end of Hayfield.

How To Pet A Dog

Tickling tummies slowly and gently works wonders. Never use a rubbing motion; this makes dogs bad-tempered. A gentle tickle with the tips of the fingers is all that is necessary to induce calm in a dog. I hate strangers who go up to dogs with their hands held to the dog's nose, usually palm towards themselves. How does the dog know that the hand doesn't hold something horrid? The palm should always be shown to the dog and go straight down to between the dog's front legs and tickle gently with a soothing voice to acompany the action. Very often the dog raises its back leg in a scratching movement, it gets so much pleasure from this.

-Barbara Woodhouse

VALLEY FORGE NATIONAL HISTORICAL PARK

THE PARK:

The most famous name in the American Revolution comes to us from a small iron forge built along Valley Creek in the 1740s. No battles were fought here, but during the winter of 1777-78, when Valley Forge grew to be the third largest city in America, hundreds of soldiers died from sickness and disease.

America's attention was redirected to long-forgotten Valley Forge during a Centennial in 1878. Preservation efforts began with Washington's Headquarters and evolved into the National Historic Park.

WALKS:

There are four marked trails, plus miles of unmarked hikes. The Multi-Use Trail loops the Colonial defensive lines and Grand Parade Ground and visits George Washington's headquarters. Sweeping field vistas of the historic grounds are found all along the trail's six-mile length. The Valley Creek Trail is a flat, linear 1.2 mile walk along Valley Creek, past the Upper Forge site. Near the Valley Creek is the eastern terminus of the 133-mile Horse-Shoe Trail; the journey to the Appalachian Trail in Hershey begins at the Artificer's Shops on Route 23. Across the Schuylkill River is the 3-mile linear Schuylkill River Trail connecting the Pawling's Parking Area and the Betzwood Picnic Area.

TRAIL TIME?

More than an hour.

TRAIL TERRAIN?

The Multi-Use Trail is gently sloping across the rolling terrain; the Valley Creek and Schuylkill River Trails are flat, waterside walks. The Horse-Shoe Trail demands a steep and strenuous climb up Mount Misery, the natural southern defender of Washington's encampment.

BONUS

You can't find a more historical dog walk than this. The Multi-Use Trail rolls past reconstructed huts and parade grounds that transport you back to the Revolution. The National Memorial Arch, a massive stone tribute dedicated in 1917, stands out along the route. The inscription reads: "Naked and starving as they are, we cannot enough admire the incomparable patience and fidelity of the soldiery. Washington at Valley Forge, February 16, 1778."

TRAIL SURFACE?

The Multi-Use Trail is paved while the others are dirt trails.

TRAIL SENSE?

A National Park Service map provides locations for the trails and does not indicate the variety of side trails available, especially from the Schuylkill River Trail. Only the Horseshoe Trail is blazed.

SWIMMING?

Valley Creek is a delightful watering hole and the Schuylkill River is easily accessed for hard-core swimming canines.

ADMISSION FEE:

None.

PARK HOURS/PHONE:

Dawn to dusk. (610.783.1000)

DIRECTIONS:

The main park entrance is on Route 23 off Route 422. Parking for the Valley Creek Trail is on Route 252 (although the Foot Bridge is washed out as of this writing). To reach the Schuylkill River Trail, exit from Route 422 onto Trooper Road, make a left and continue back across Route 422 to the Betzwood Picnic Area or cross the Schuylkill River on Pawlings Road from Route 23 at the other end. Parking for trails here is on the right side across the bridge and also up the road at Walnut Hill.

WARWICK COUNTY PARK

THE PARK:

The woodlands in Warwick County Park's 455 acres provided much of the timber for charcoal used in the American iron industry. The land was an original grant to Samuel Nutt in 1718, who took to mining the property. By 1738 the Warwick Furnace was established and it was to be one of the most substantial in the American colonies. The first Franklin Stove was cast here and the Warwick Cannon helped win the Revolution. Charcoal hearths chiseled into the steep slopes can still be seen flanking some trails. The park was dedicated in 1973.

WALKS:

The premier walk in Warwick is the Charcoal Trail Loop, a narrow, rocky, mile-long loop up and down the slopes of the French Creek Valley. The North Loop Trail, designed like a long lasso, is a pleasant woods-and-field walk, much of it on the old bed of the Sowbelly Railroad. Two of the Horse-Shoe Trail's 133 miles bisect the park and there is a 1/2-mile Adirondack Trail where you can test your ability to identify the trees and shrubs commonly found in an Eastern hardwood forest. The trail access from the Coventry Road parking lot is overgrown and provides access only to the French Creek South Branch, but not the rest of the park.

TRAIL TIME?

More than one hour.

TRAIL TERRAIN?

There are many long stretches of flat terrain and easy walking but the Charcoal Trail will give your dog a cardiac workout.

TRAIL SURFACE?

Mostly dirt trails through the trees.

BONUS

In 1850 Albert Fink, a German railroad engineer, designed and patented a bridge that used a latticework of rods instead of cables to reinforce stiffness. This construction was cheap and sturdy, making the Fink Truss one of the most commonly used railroad bridges in the 1860s, especially favored by the powerful Baltimore & Ohio Railroad, Only one Fink Truss bridge remains in the United States - an abandoned 108-foot span in Zoarsville, Ohio. A wooden reproduction of a Fink Truss is in a field at Warwick County Park for you and your dog to climb.

TRAIL SENSE?

The trails are blazed, save for the North Loop, and a trail map is available.

SWIMMING?

There is very little water at Warwick; none at all along the Charcoal Trail and minimal access to the French Creek elsewhere. There is, however, a pretty, fleeting encounter with the creek on the North Loop, west of the Conifer Field.

ADMISSION FEE:

None.

PARK HOURS/PHONE:

8:00 a.m. - sunset, year-round. (610.469.1916)

DIRECTIONS:

Warwick County Park is in Knauertown, on Route 23, four miles west of Route 100. The main park entrance is located on County Park Road and parking for the North Loop Trail is on Mt. Pleasant Road, east of the main entrance.

A door is what a dog is perpetually on the wrong side of.

-James Thurber

WELKINWEIR

THE PARK:

Welkinweir ("where sky meets water") was a foundering farm during the Depression when the property was purchased by Everett and Grace Rodebaugh. The Rodebaughs reintroduced native trees and meadows and constructed a series of ponds in the valley beneath the farmhouse.

In 1964, Everett Rodebaugh founded the Green Valleys Association to protect five watersheds draining 151 square miles of northern Chester County. In 1997 the Rodebaughs conveyed Welkinweir to the Green Valleys Association for use as a headquarters and eduational center.

WALKS:

A woodland trail loops around the 162-acre nature sanctuary, leading through wetlands, ponds, and meadows. The trail through the back of the property can be narrow and overgrown. For longer walks, the Welkinweir trail features a short connector to the Horse-Shoe Trail, which skirts the property on two sides.

TRAIL TIME?

More than one hour.

TRAIL TERRAIN?

This is hilly property, especially in the backstretch of the loop.

TRAIL SURFACE?

Mostly dirt trails through the trees. Some of the meadow trails are shaved stalks which are rough on your pet's paws.

TRAIL SENSE?

The West Trail Entrance begins at the parking lot and the trail is blazed in white. It is not a complete loop and there is a property map available to navigate through the developed areas.

BONUS
There are dramatic vistas from the garden areas around the property. As one visitor commented in the Welkinweir guest book: "It's a Grand Canyon of trees!"

SWIMMING?

Although the West Branch of Beaver Run is not deep enough for doggie dipping, it engorges into several ponds on the property.

ADMISSION FEE:

Adults, 17 and up - $5.00; Youths (4-16) - $3.00.

PARK HOURS/PHONE:

9:00 a.m. - dusk. (610.469.4900)

DIRECTIONS:

Welkinweir is west of Phoenixville. From the intersection of Routes 23 and 100, take Route 100 south for 1.1 miles. Make a right on Prizer Road. Follow for .8 a mile to Welkinweir on the left. The Visitor Entrance is the second of three access points and is marked by a sign.

Best Parks To Hike More Than An Hour With The Dog

1. French Creek State Park
2. White Clay Creek Preserve
3. Valley Forge National Historical Park
4. State Game Lands No. 43
5. Hibernia County Park

WHITE CLAY CREEK PRESERVE/ WHITE CLAY CREEK STATE PARK

THE PARK:

William Penn bought most of this land in 1683 from Lenni Lenape Chief Kekelappen. Kekelappen was believed to have lived here in Opasiskunk, an "Indian Town" at the confluence of the middle and east branches of the White Clay Creek in the center of the preserve. Of the many Lenni-Lenape Indian Towns in what is now Chester County, this was considered the most important. Frequent flooding over the past three centuries has obliterated all evidence of this former large settlement. In 1984 the DuPont Company donated the land which would become the 1,253-acre preserve. Many of the old structures from the early days of settlement are still visible. Another 2,300 acres adjoin the preserve in Delaware's White Clay Creek State Park.

WALKS:

The Penndel Trail, over three miles in length, is a superb linear trail which follows the east branch of the White Clay Creek, crosses the Middle Branch and continues along the main waterway into White Clay Creek State Park in Delaware. There are also eight miles of bridle trails across the fields and on the opposite side of the stream.

TRAIL TIME?

More than an hour.

TRAIL TERRAIN?

The walks are flat along the creek but there are plenty of hills elsewhere, especially if you continue into Delaware.

TRAIL SURFACE?

Dirt, with stretches of sand and rocks underfoot. The horse trails are often grass-covered. The trails are almost universally wide.

BONUS

In the southern part of the preserve is the Arc Corner Monument marking one end of the 12-mile arc which forms the Pennsylvania-Delaware state line, unique in American political boundary-making. The circular divide dates to William Penn's directive of August 28, 1701, when Delaware was still a part of Pennsylvania, known as the Lower Three Counties. A little more than 1/2 mile to the west is another monument marking the tri-state junction of Delaware,Pennsylvania and Maryland.

TRAIL SENSE?

The Penndel Trail (also the Mason-Dixon Trail in the preserve) is blazed in blue and a trail map is available.

SWIMMING?

There are many excellent swimming holes in the White Clay Creek.

ADMISSION FEE:

None. The White Clay Creek State Park in Delaware charges a daily fee from Memorial Day to Labor Day and weekends in May, September and October.

PARK HOURS/PHONE:

8:00 a.m. - sunset, year-round. (610.274-2900)

DIRECTIONS:

White Clay Creek Preserve is in southeastern Chester County. From Route 896 (New London Road) make a left on London Tract Road. The office is at the junction of London tract and Sharpless Roads. Parking Lot 1, further up London Tract Road, is the northern terminus for the Penndel Trail.

Parks Nearby

ANDORRA NATURAL AREA/ FAIRMOUNT PARK

Philadelphia County, Pennsylvania

THE PARK:

America's first public park began with 5 acres in 1812. Today, Fairmount Park is the largest contiguous landscaped municipal park in the world with nearly 9,000 acres. It is home to an estimated 2,500,000 trees.

The Andorra Natural Area, at the park's northern boundary with Montgomery County, evolved from a 19th century nursery. Ownership of the property dates to 1840 when Richard Wistar named it "Andorra" from a Moorish word meaning "hills covered with trees." One of those trees - a massive sycamore - grew right through an enclosed porch in the house of the chief plant propagator of the nursery. The weakening sycamore was cut down in 1981 but the Tree House survives as the Andorra Visitor Center.

WALKS:

The main trail at Andorra is a 20-station Nature hike. There are also a dozen other short named trails that branch off this trail. The Forbidden Drive also begins its 7-mile journey along the Wissahickon Creek to the Schuylkill River here. The Forbidden Drive, so-named when it was closed to automobiles in the 1920s, can be shortened by several bridges across the Wissahickon for the return trip. There are also many blazed trails climbing out of the Wissahickon Gorge from the Forbidden Drive.

BONUS

In 1855, a hotel entrepreneur built a new inn on Rex Avenue. To draw attention to his hostelry he constructed an Indian from old barn boards and propped it up on top of a rock overlooking the Gorge. In 1902, when the Indian Rock Hotel was long gone but with the silhouette still there, artist Massey Rhind was commissioned to make a representation of a "Delaware Indian, looking west to where his people have gone." The kneeling warrior has gazed up the Wissahickon Gorge ever since. A switchback trail leads to the Indian Statue where you can get close enough to pat his knee. And take in a breathtaking view.

TRAIL TIME?

More than an hour.

TRAIL TERRAIN?

The Forbidden Drive is flat; although the climbs out of the forested Wissahickon Gorge are steep, the trails are relatively easy walking once the task is completed.

TRAIL SURFACE?

The Forbidden Drive is compacted gravel; the woodland trails are dirt and rocks.

TRAIL SENSE?

The paths are blazed and a map of Andorra is available.

SWIMMING?

The swimming is excellent in the Wissahickon Creek.

ADMISSION FEE:

None.

PARK HOURS/PHONE:

5:00 a.m. - 1:00 a.m., year-round. (215-685-9285)

DIRECTIONS:

Andorra is on Northwestern Avenue between Ridge Avenue and Germantown Avenue.

BRANDYWINE CREEK STATE PARK

New Castle County, Delaware

THE PARK:

Once a du Pont family dairy farm, this spectacular tract of land became a State Park in 1965. Delaware's first two nature preserves are here: Tulip Tree Woods, behind the park office with majestic trees over 200 years old, and Freshwater Marsh, at the edge of the Brandywine Creek. The stone walls that criss-cross the 850-acre park are the legacy of skilled Italian masons who crafted the barriers from locally quarried Brandywine granite, the original "Wilmington Blue Rocks."

WALKS:

There are 8 blazed trails on both sides of the Brandywine. All are short, all are woodsy and all are hilly. The star walk at Thompson's Bridge is the rugged Rocky Run Trail, winding around the closest thing to a mountain stream in Delaware. Also at Thompson's Bridge is a Multi-Use Trail that follows the Brandywine Creek for about two miles. You can walk the dog across the Brandywine at Thompson's Bridge via a short, unmarked trail at the end of the boardwalk through Hidden Pond that leads to the roadway.

TRAIL TIME?

More than an hour.

TRAIL TERRAIN?

If you can't reach out and touch the water of the Brandywine you are moving up or down a hill.

TRAIL SURFACE?

Dirt; the Multi-Use Trail is embedded with rocks.

TRAIL SENSE?

All the paths are blazed and there is an excellent color map available.

BONUS

In the winter of 1802 a rudderless French immigrant living in New Jersey named Eleuthere Irenee du Pont was invited to the Brandywine Valley to hunt game. It was not a successful trip. The damp weather fouled his gunpowder and his musket continually misfired. It was so bad du Pont decided to re-enter the industry he had turned his back on in France as a youth: black powder. When it came time to launch his new business he remembered what you see today at Brandywine Creek State Park: the hardwood forests that would burn to charcoal, one of the ingredients he would need for powder; the abundant granite in the hills to build his mills; and the swift-flowing river to power the mills. And so he returned to Delaware to launch an empire. Incidentally, the favorite breed of dog for the du Pont family when they lived here: the greyhound.

SWIMMING?

The Brandywine Creek is one of the best places in Delaware to take your dog for a swim.

ADMISSION FEE:

Charged daily from Memorial Day-Labor Day and weekends in May, September and October.

PARK HOURS/PHONE:

8:00 a.m. - sunset, year-round. (302.577.3534)

DIRECTIONS:

The main entrance is on Adams Dam Road, between Thompson's Bridge Road (Route 92) and Rockland Road. Another parking areas is at Thompson's Bridge Road.

FAIR HILL NATURAL RESOURCES MANAGEMENT AREA

Cecil County, Maryland

THE PARK:

This is the Godzilla of area hiking. Traversing its 5,613 acres are over 75 miles of multi-use trails. Many go through rolling hayfields as befits its stature as a leading equine training center.

WALKS:

The trails through the fields are typically doubletrack (old dirt vehicle roads). Singletrack trails dominate in the forested areas. The Big Elk Creek surges through the property and is spanned by many trail bridges, including one of Maryland's five remaining covered bridges. The Big Elk Creek Covered Bridge was built in 1860 at a cost of $1,165. When it was reconstructed in 1992 after sustaining extensive damage from heavy trucks, the tab was $152,000.

TRAIL TIME?

More than an hour.

TRAIL TERRAIN?

The stiffest climbs are in the vicinity of the Big Elk Creek but most of the trails are like walking a steeplechase course.

TRAIL SURFACE?

Mostly natural trails, usually dirt.

TRAIL SENSE?

The trails are not marked and there are times you can feel like a real explorer when you leave the doubletrack trails. Unless you enjoy that feeling all day, which many do, a trail map from the office is mandatory. Be aware - there are more dead ends here than in an English maze garden.

BONUS

Flying concentric circles outward from Philadelphia, Hollywood location scouts for Oprah Winfrey's movie project, *Beloved*, spotted the Fair Hill terrain and selected it as the backdrop for the film's rural scenes. A ramshackle 19th-century tenant farm was constructed and much of the movie shot here. The producers decided to leave the movie set intact, to deteriorate naturally. You can wander among the fake buildings and even knock on the styrofoam stones.

SWIMMING?

The Big Elk Creek runs swift and shallow through the park - deep enough for trout but not for dogs.

ADMISSION FEE:

$2 parking fee.

PARK HOURS:

Sunrise - sunset, year-round.

DIRECTIONS:

Fair Hill is just west of Newark. Take Route 273 across the Maryland-Delaware State line until the first four-way intersection, Appleton Road, about 1.2 miles. There is parking down either side of Appleton Road. The park office is on Route 273, behind the grandstands for the Fair Hill Race Track.

The greatest pleasure of a dog is that you may make a fool of yourself with him, and not only will he not scold you, but will make a fool of himself too.

-Samuel Butler

JOHN HEINZ NATIONAL WILDLIFE REFUGE AT TINICUM

Philadelphia County, Pennsylvania

THE PARK:

There are more than 500 National Wildlife Refuges in the United States and only Philadelphia and San Francisco offer an urban environmental study. When the Swedes settled here in 1634, Tinicum Marsh measured over 5,700 acres. Three hundred years later the tidal marsh had been reduced to only 200 acres. The routing of I-95 in 1969 threatened to finish off the marsh but, in ironic fact, saved it. Congress authorized the purchase of 1,200 acres in 1972, establishing the Tinicum National Environmental Center and enabling the highway to roar through the area.

WALKS:

You can cover about ten miles of trails here in two major loops. The more attractive of the two is around the Impoundment marsh near the Visitor Contact Station. If you have a patient dog you can pause at the Observation Platform or one of the Observation Blinds and try to identify one of the 288 species of birds seen in the refuge.

The western loop, which begins in Delaware County, leads onto a dike in the middle of the marsh and along the Darby Creek. The trail on the dike is narrow to the point of being overgrown during the spring and summer.

TRAIL TIME?

More than an hour.

TRAIL TERRAIN?

Flat everywhere.

TRAIL SURFACE?

Dirt and grass, with long stretches of gravel road.

BONUS

There aren't many other places where you can walk along and scan the skies alternately for a Northern Goshawk and a McDonnell-Douglas or a Buff-Breasted Sandpiper and a Boeing.

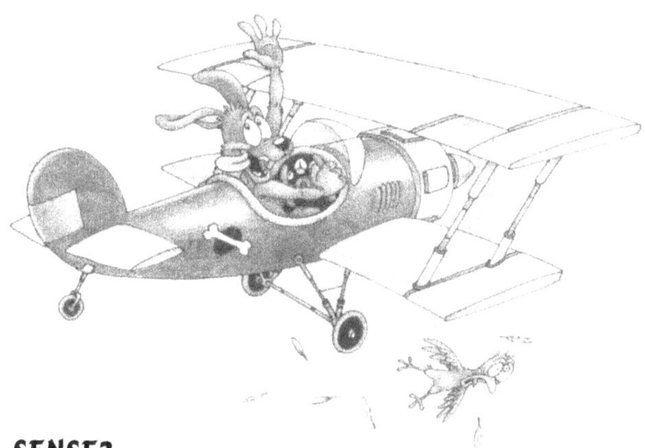

TRAIL SENSE?

The trail is not marked nor blazed but there is a map available. It is not detailed and expect to take a detour or two near the Route 420 parking area. Also, when walking along I-95, keep to the highway side of the chain link fence.

SWIMMING?

The Darby Creek is accessible but the fish pulled from these waters are contaminated so you may want to limit water time here.

ADMISSION FEE:

None.

PARK HOURS/PHONE:

8:00 a.m. - sunset, year-round. (215.365.3118)

DIRECTIONS:

Take I-95 North. Take Exit 10, Route 291 (Philadelphia International Airport). At the first light make a left onto Bartram Avenue. At the third light make a left onto 84th Street. At the second light make a left onto Lindbergh Boulevard. Make a right into the refuge just past the stop sign. There is also a parking area on Route 420; take Exit 9B for Route 420 North. The parking area is right there.

RIDLEY CREEK STATE PARK

Delaware County, Pennsylvania

THE PARK:

Settlement in this area dates back to the 1600s when villages grew around the mills sprinkled along the creeks and streams. Much of the park's 2,606 acres were consolidated in the Jefford's family - their "Hunting Hill" mansion, built in 1914 around a 1789 stone farmhouse, now serves as the park office. The commonwealth of Pennsylvania purchased the property in the 1960s - including 35 historic residences - and the park was dedicated in 1972.

WALKS:

Ridley Creek features 12 miles of hiking on four main trails. The White Trail visits most of the areas of the park and the others intersect this loop trail at many points. At its southern end the Yellow Trail connects with the trails of the adjacent Tyler Arboretum. A 5-mile multi-use loop is shared with bicyclists and joggers. Also, an unmarked trailhead just east of Ridley Creek on Gradyville Road offers one of the longest creekside walks in the area. CAUTION: These heavily wooded trails are narrow in many places and you and the dog will be prime targets for hitchhiking ticks.

TRAIL TIME?

More than an hour.

TRAIL TERRAIN?

Most of the trails wind through rolling woodland and meadows. You will be moving up and down often but only an occasional hardy climb is necessary.

TRAIL SURFACE?

Mostly dirt; the multi-use trail is paved.

BONUS

Along the multi-use trail are metal doggie water bowls chained to the benches.

TRAIL SENSE?

The trails are blazed and easy to follow, except through the parking areas - keep your eye on the pavement here. A trail map is available.

SWIMMING?

Ridley Creek, while extremely scenic, is a relatively minor feature of hiking at Ridley Creek State Park. It is deep enough for swimming when the trail touches upon it. There are no ponds on the property.

ADMISSION FEE:

None.

PARK HOURS/PHONE:

8 a.m. - sunset, year-round. (610.892.3900)

DIRECTIONS:

The park can be accessed from Route 3, 2.5 miles west of Newtown Square, past the Colonial Pennsylvania Plantation. The park may also be entered from Gradyville Road - east from Route 352 or west from Route 252.

SCOTT ARBORETUM

Delaware County, Pennsylvania

THE PARK:

The 300-acre Swarthmore campus is developed to be an arboretum, established in 1929 as a living memorial to Arthur Hoyt Scott, Class of 1895. The 3,000 different kinds of plants have been chosen as suggestions for the best trees, shrubs, perennials and annuals to use in home gardens in the Delaware Valley.

WALKS:

Several area colleges welcome responsible dog owners - Swarthmore's Scott Arboretum is the best walk. The collections are integrated with the stone buildings of the college which dates to 1864. There are also trails through the 200-acre Crum Woods, where your dog need only be under voice control. You'll find dog water bowls at the drinking fountains here, too.

TRAIL TIME?

More than an hour.

TRAIL TERRAIN?

The walk around campus is level; Crum Woods is situated on a steep hillside.

TRAIL SURFACE?

All the surfaces on campus are paved. The trails in Crum Woods are mostly dirt but can also be broken macadam and stone.

TRAIL SENSE?

There are no trail markings but a detailed campus map is available.

SWIMMING?

Crum Creek is deep enough to permit canine swimming.

BONUS

In the far southwestern area of campus, beyond the holly collection, is a meadow containing a Swarthmore version of Stonehenge. Like the original, its origins are mysterious. From the slate bench you can chance to see the SEPTA trolley rolling over a 50-foot trestle across Crum Creek.

ADMISSION FEE:

None.

PARK HOURS/PHONE:

Dawn to dusk, year-round. (610.328.8025)

DIRECTIONS:

The Scott Arboretum is in Swarthmore on Chester Road (Route 320) between I-95 and Baltimore Pike. Parking for the Scott Arboretum is just inside the entrance on College Road, on the left.

www.ingramcontent.com/pod-product-compliance
Lightning Source LLC
LaVergne TN
LVHW010544100826
845148LV00013B/2591

* 9 7 8 0 9 6 4 4 4 2 7 3 3 *